Creatures and Cryptids:

An Adult Coloring Book

Pictures and words by

Nathan T. Wright

ISBN 978-1543139174

Introduction

Oh hi there! I hope you enjoy mythical beasts and otherworldly monsters as much as I do. (This book, as you've probably figured out, is full of them.)

My obsession with creatures and cryptids started when I was a kid hanging out at the public library. Books about Bigfoot, Nessie and UFOs were my go-to reading material. If the subject matter was mysterious, weird and unexplained, I was into it.

The artwork inside the books fascinated me. Detailed illustrations of monsters cobbled together from blurry photos and eyewitness accounts sent my imagination into overdrive. I haven't stopped drawing mermaids, sea serpents and ape-men since.

This coloring book is a celebration of creatures that exist on the fringes of biology and forever elude documentation. You'll see some familiar faces and a few from my own imagination.
I hope you enjoy it.

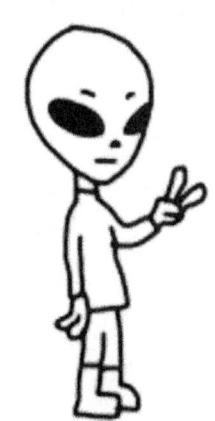

- Nathan

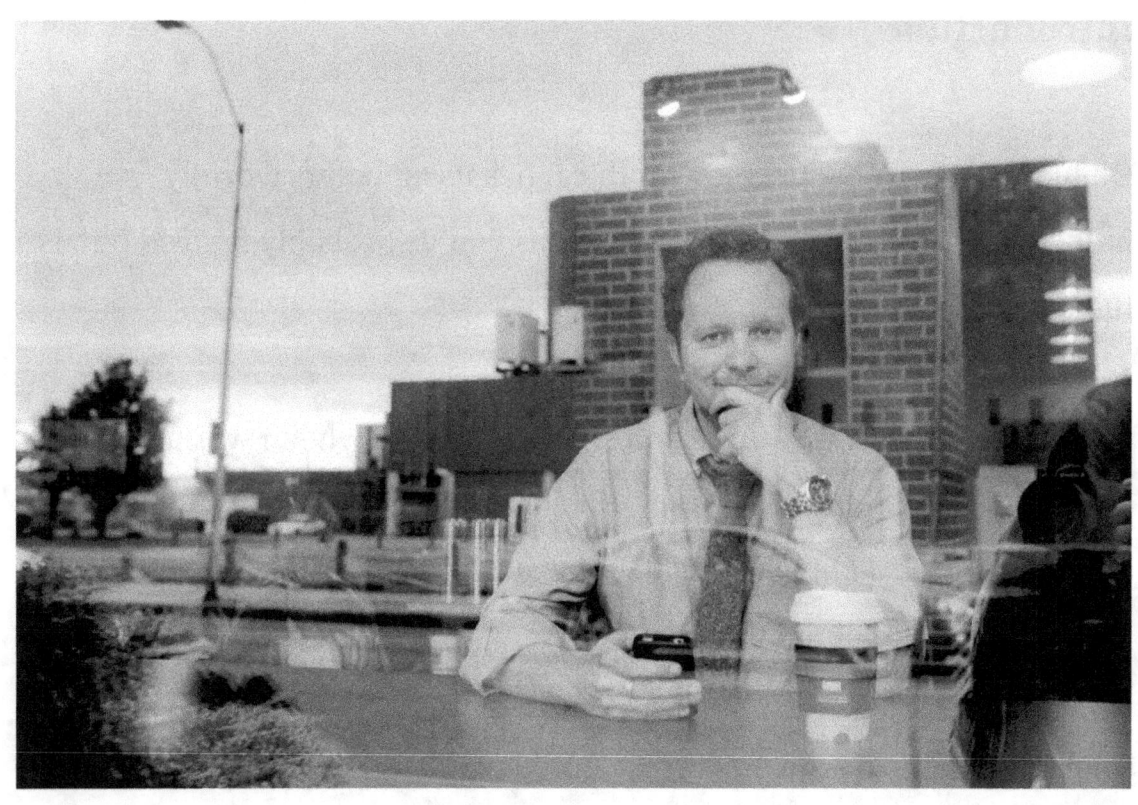

Nathan T. Wright is an artist based in Des Moines, Iowa, specializing in custom illustration projects, prints and books. His work is inspired by sci-fi, comics, emerging tech, animation, cartoon strips and the occasional glass of whiskey.

Visit him online at nathantwright.com.

Try to find these things while you're hunting for monsters.

They're hidden throughout the book.

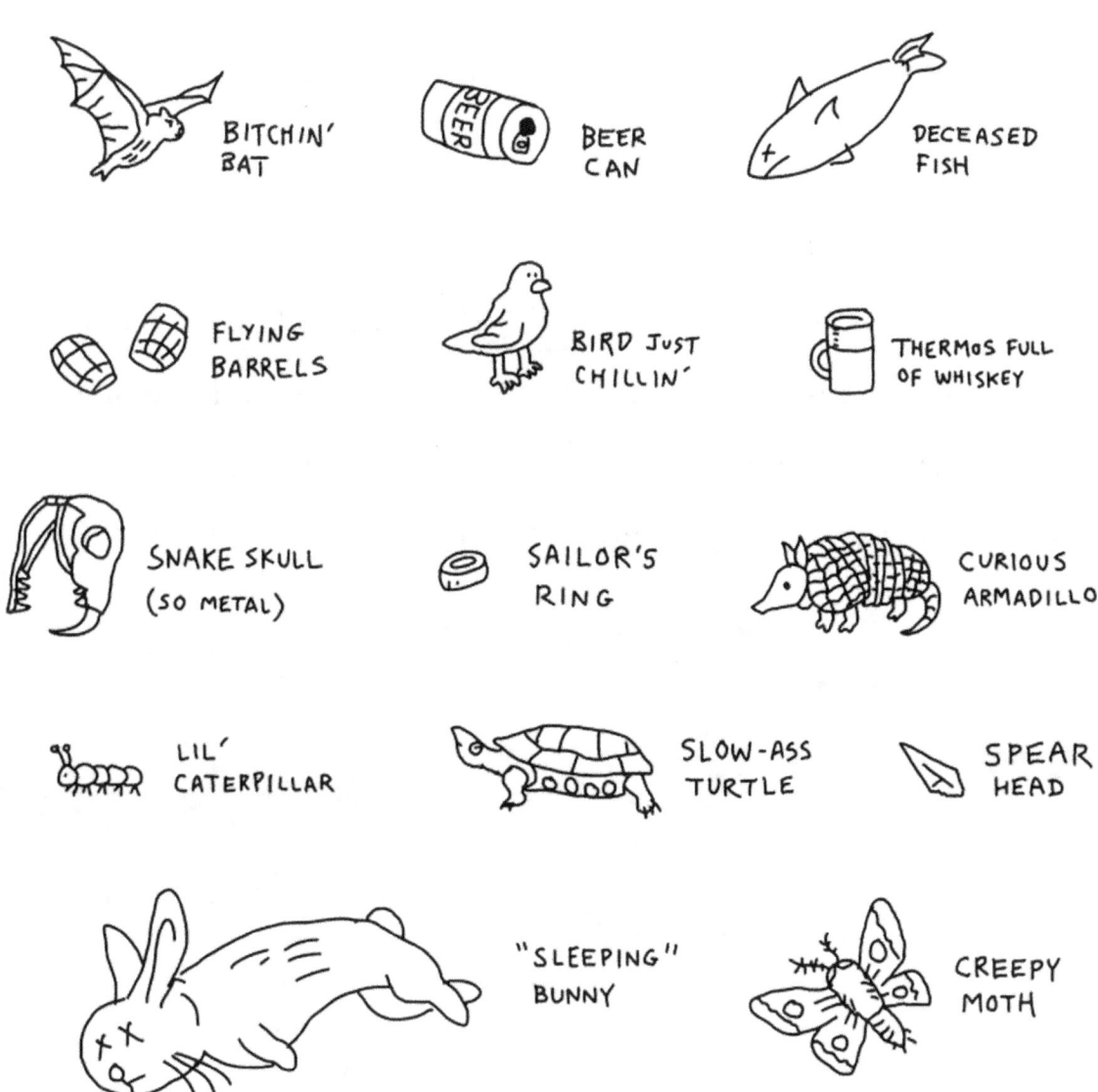

BITCHIN' BAT

BEER CAN

DECEASED FISH

FLYING BARRELS

BIRD JUST CHILLIN'

THERMOS FULL OF WHISKEY

SNAKE SKULL (SO METAL)

SAILOR'S RING

CURIOUS ARMADILLO

LIL' CATERPILLAR

SLOW-ASS TURTLE

SPEAR HEAD

"SLEEPING" BUNNY

CREEPY MOTH

Bigfoot

The best thing about Bigfoot isn't his hirsute nature or his determined, arm-swinging gait; it's all of his various names. The hairy creature is known by as many names as there are cultures. Here are just a few: Sasquatch, Yowie, Yeti, Alma, Wendigo and my personal favorite – the Skunk Ape!

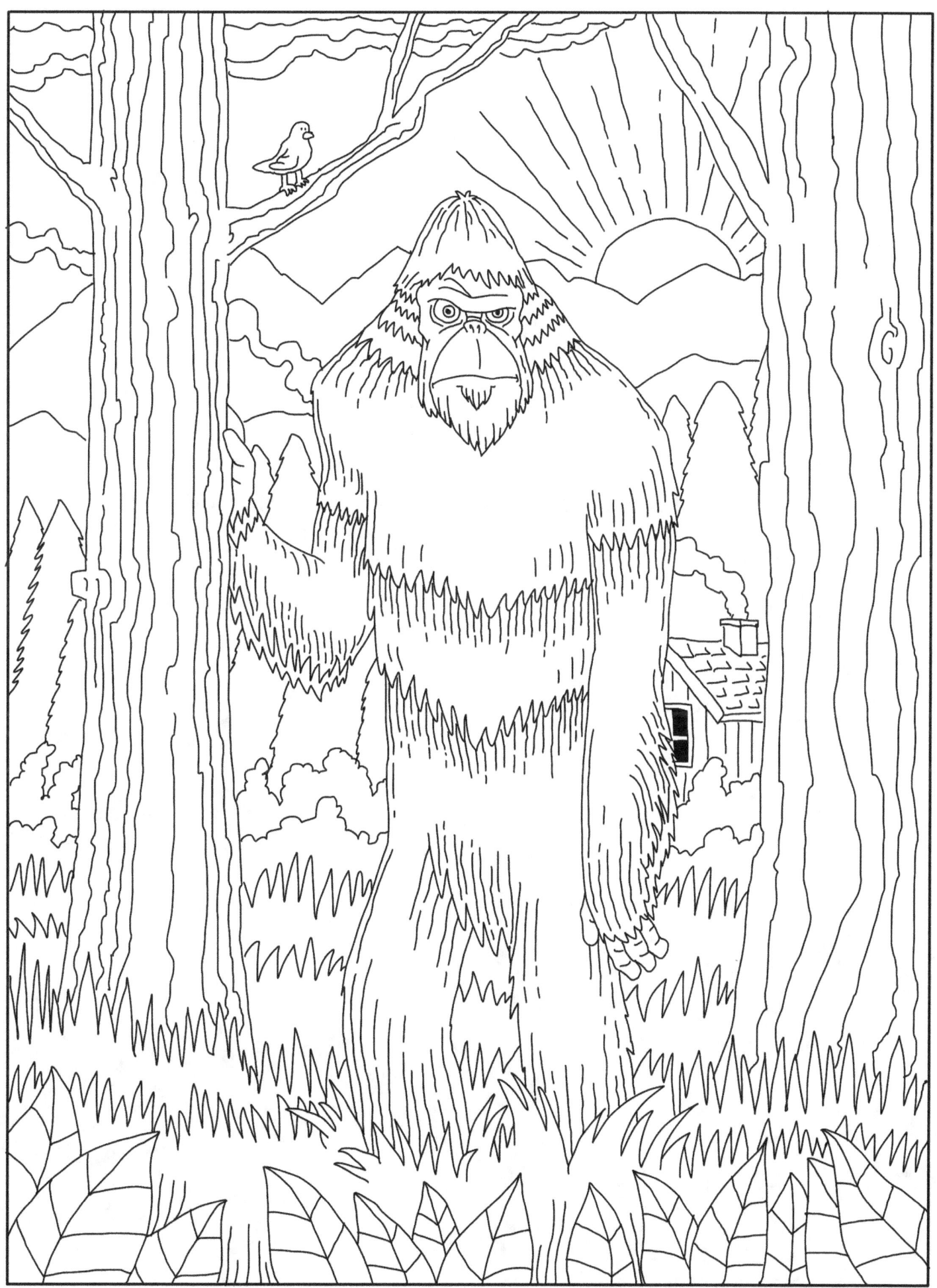

The Loch Ness Monster

There are lots of logical explanations for Loch Ness Monster sightings: bird wakes, seals, swimming deer, floating logs, even seismic gas. I prefer the "plesiosaur trapped in a freshwater loch" theory, myself.

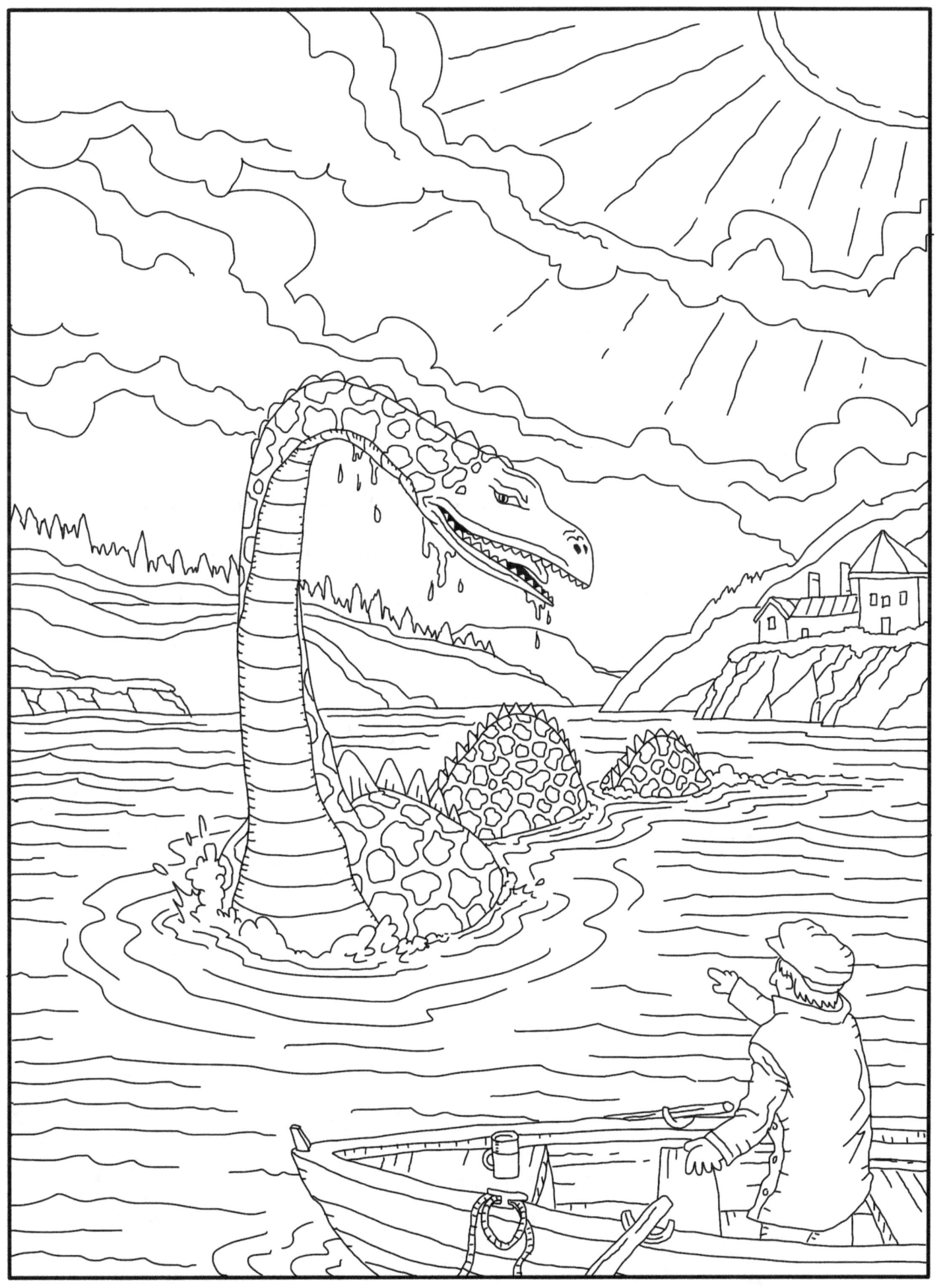

The Jersey Devil

Those who claim to have seen the Jersey Devil describe a creature with a kangaroo-like body, hooves, antlers, bat wings and – just to make sure everything seems plausible – a goat's head. Additionally, it is the only mythical creature to have an NHL franchise named after it.

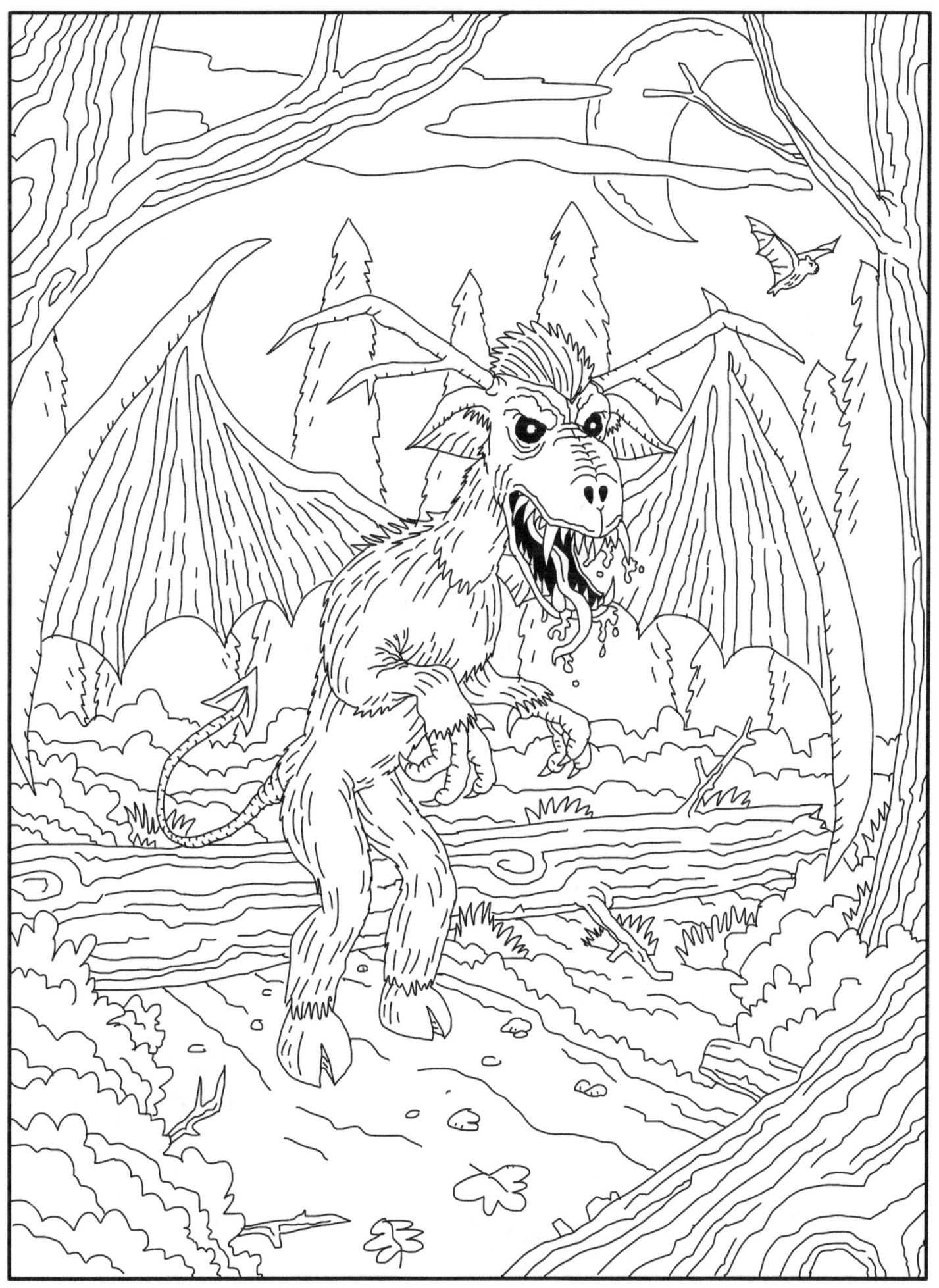

Mermaids

Christopher Columbus reported some of the earliest mermaid sightings during his exploration of the Caribbean, although they were probably just manatees. Columbus was also an awful human being and mass murderer, so let's not rely on his judgment. Mermaids were likely adopted from the Sirens of Greek mythology, known for luring sailors to their deaths with their spellbinding voices and music.

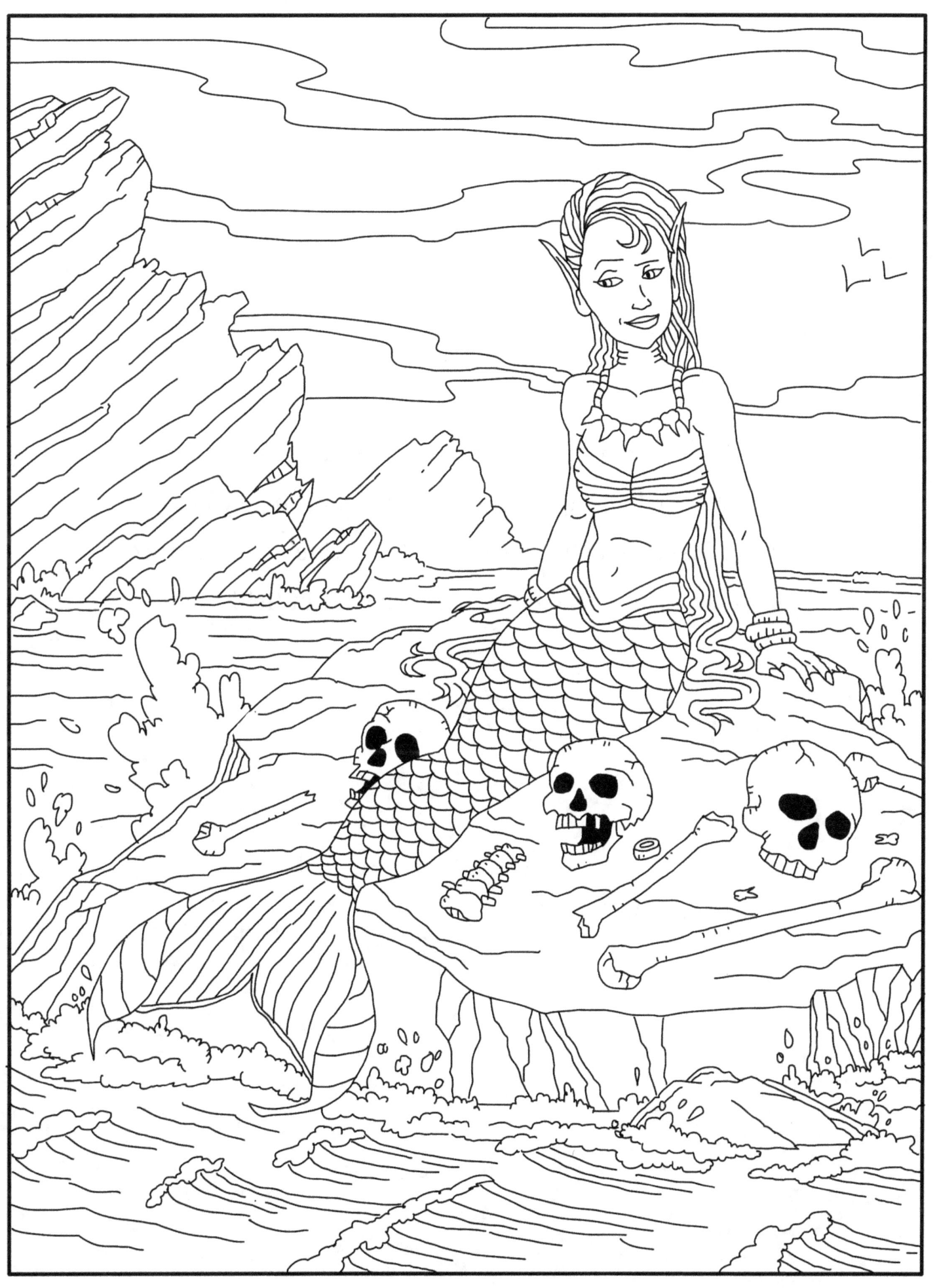

The Griffin

The Griffin is the most majestic and powerful of all the beasts because it's one-half eagle, one-half lion. I challenge you to find a more badass animal hybrid. Gator-Wolverine? Wolf-Cobra? Gorilla-Shark? Ha! Those things don't exist! But Griffins do.

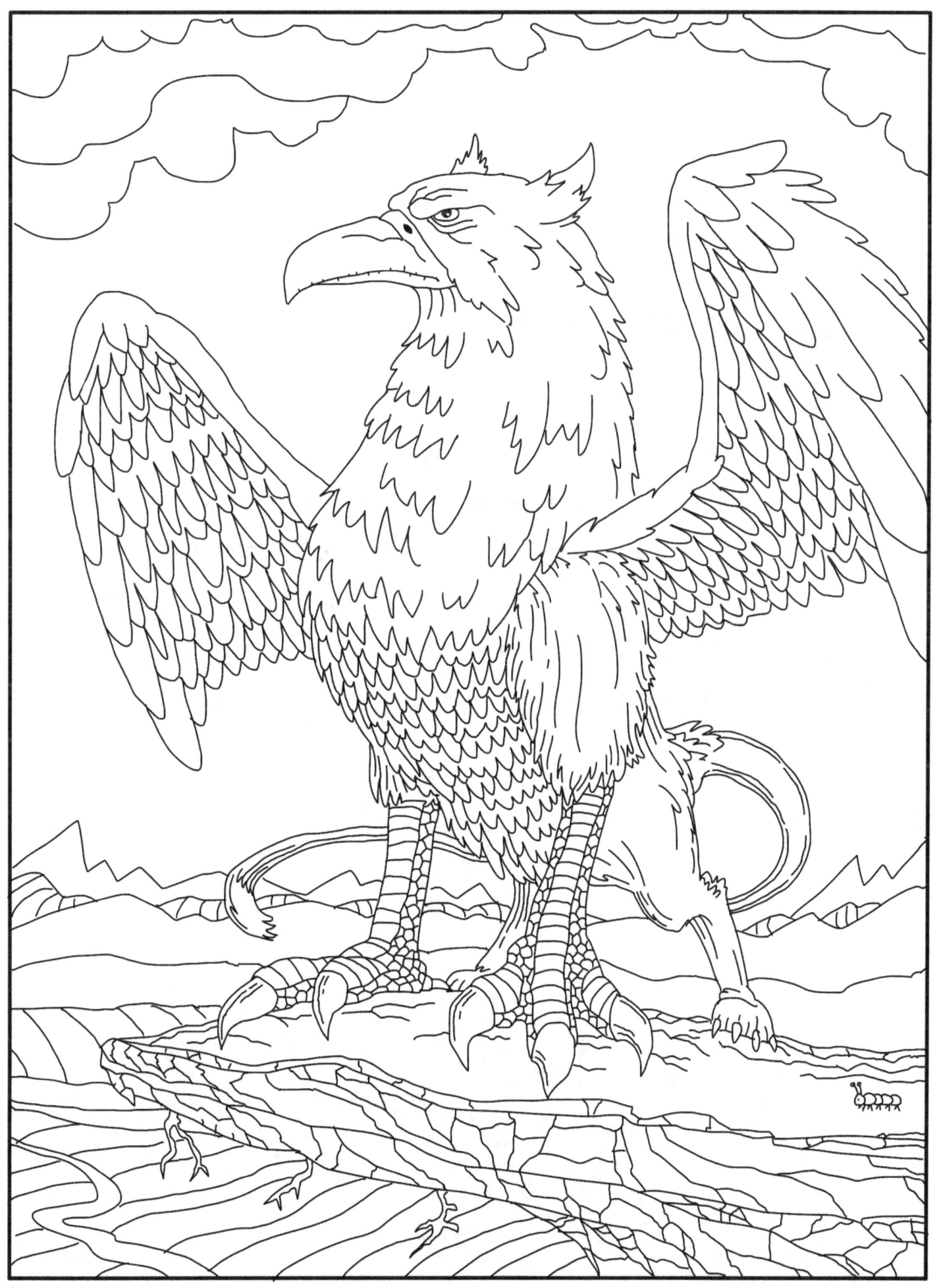

Swamp Monsters

Louisiana is known for all sorts of spooky things like creepy old antebellum homes, moss-covered Cypress trees and haunted bayous. But don't forget about the leech-infested swamps, home to mythical Swamp Monsters! These creatures mostly live underwater and only surface when provoked. So don't provoke them.

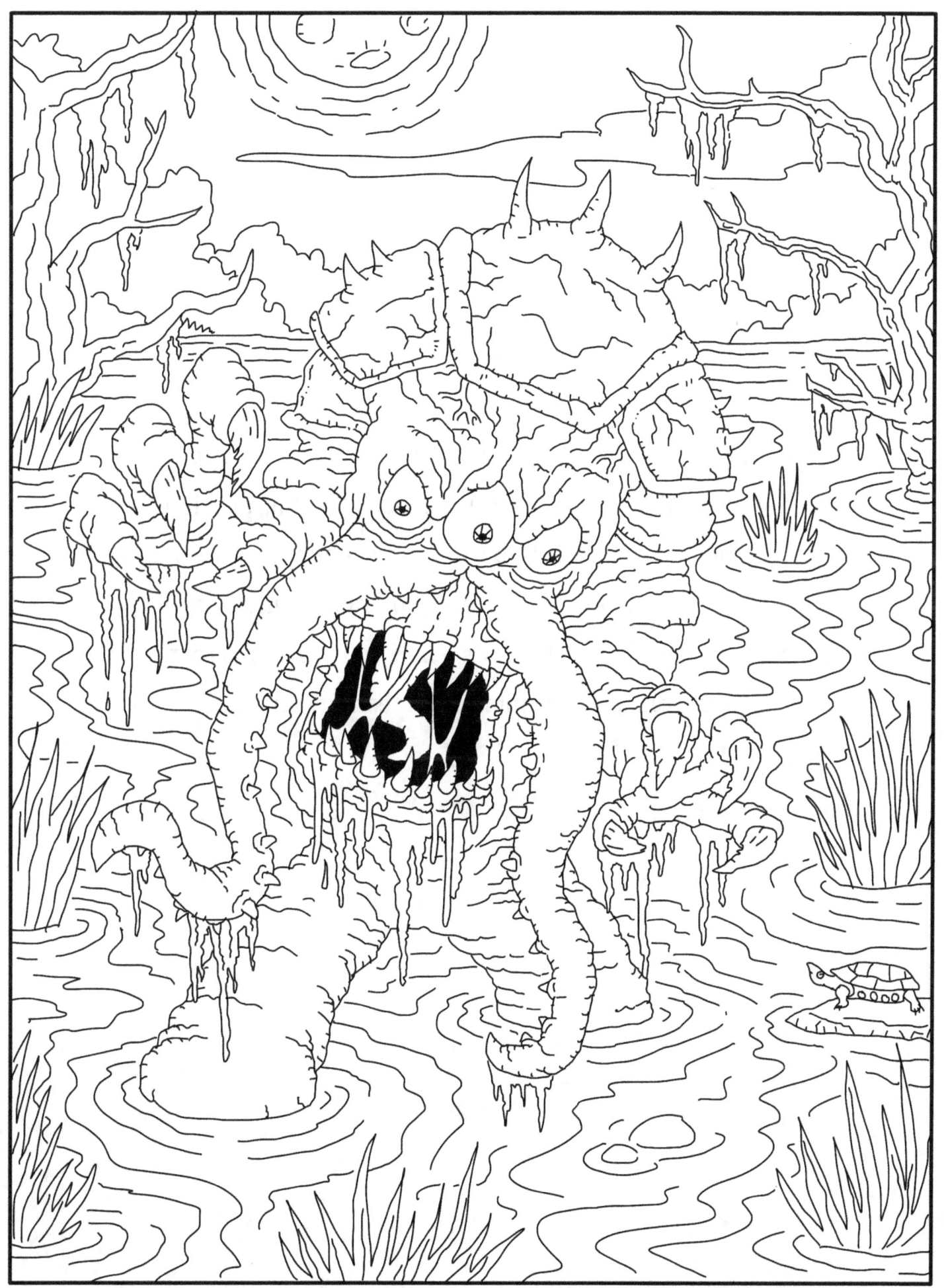

Pig-Man

Some nights there are terrible noises outside my bedroom window. Gnashing of teeth, grunting, flesh tearing, snarling, snorting, bones snapping. And sometimes I hear giggling and oinking. Logic tells me it's just a raccoon murdering a small rodent. However I've decided it's a half man, half pig creature that escaped from a government DNA testing facility.

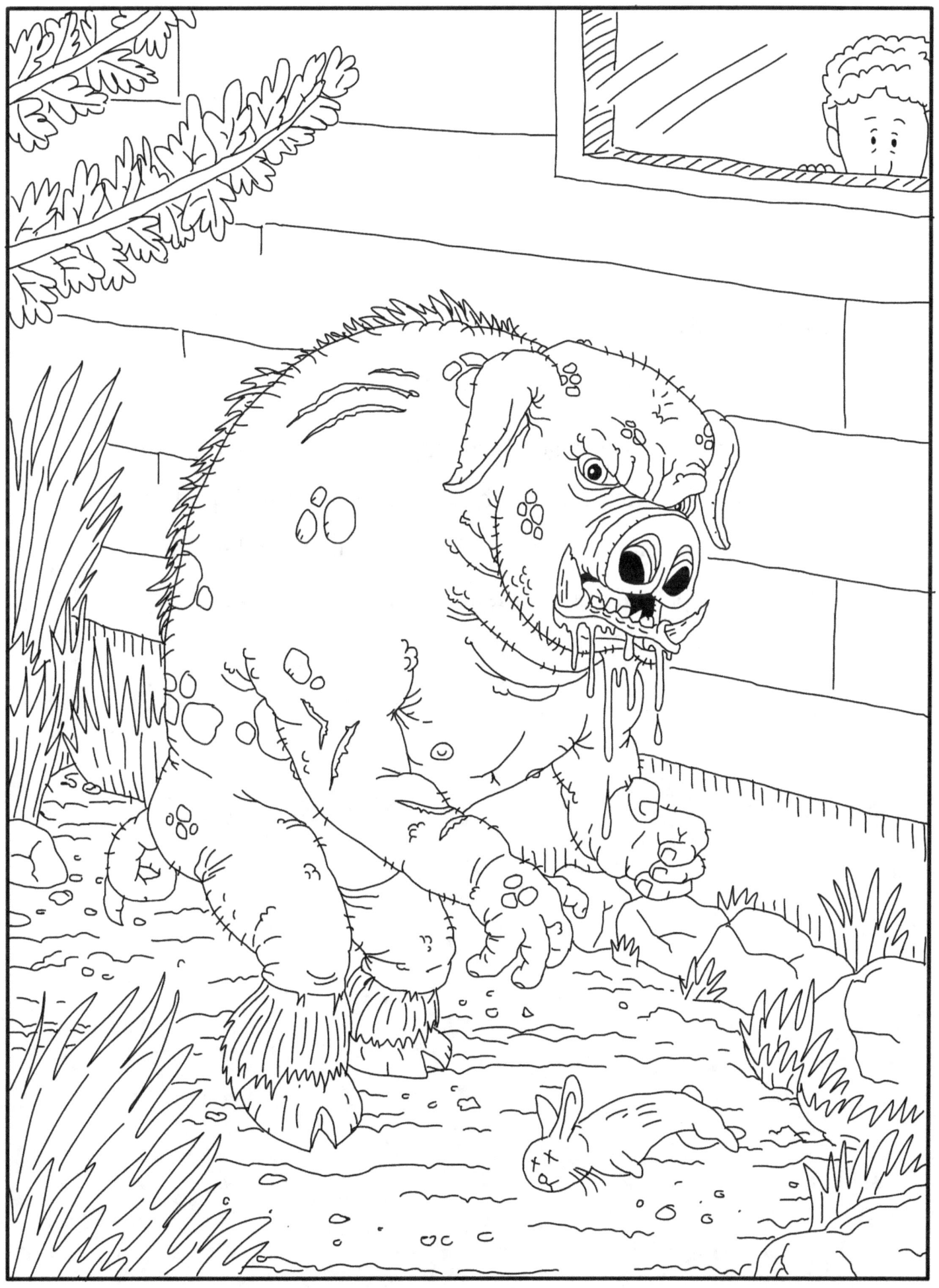

The Kraken

Of all the sea monster legends throughout human history, there is evidence that the Kraken is based on a real cephalopod – the Giant Squid. But it's more fun to imagine supersized tentacles attacking ships and pulling them down into the ocean's depths.

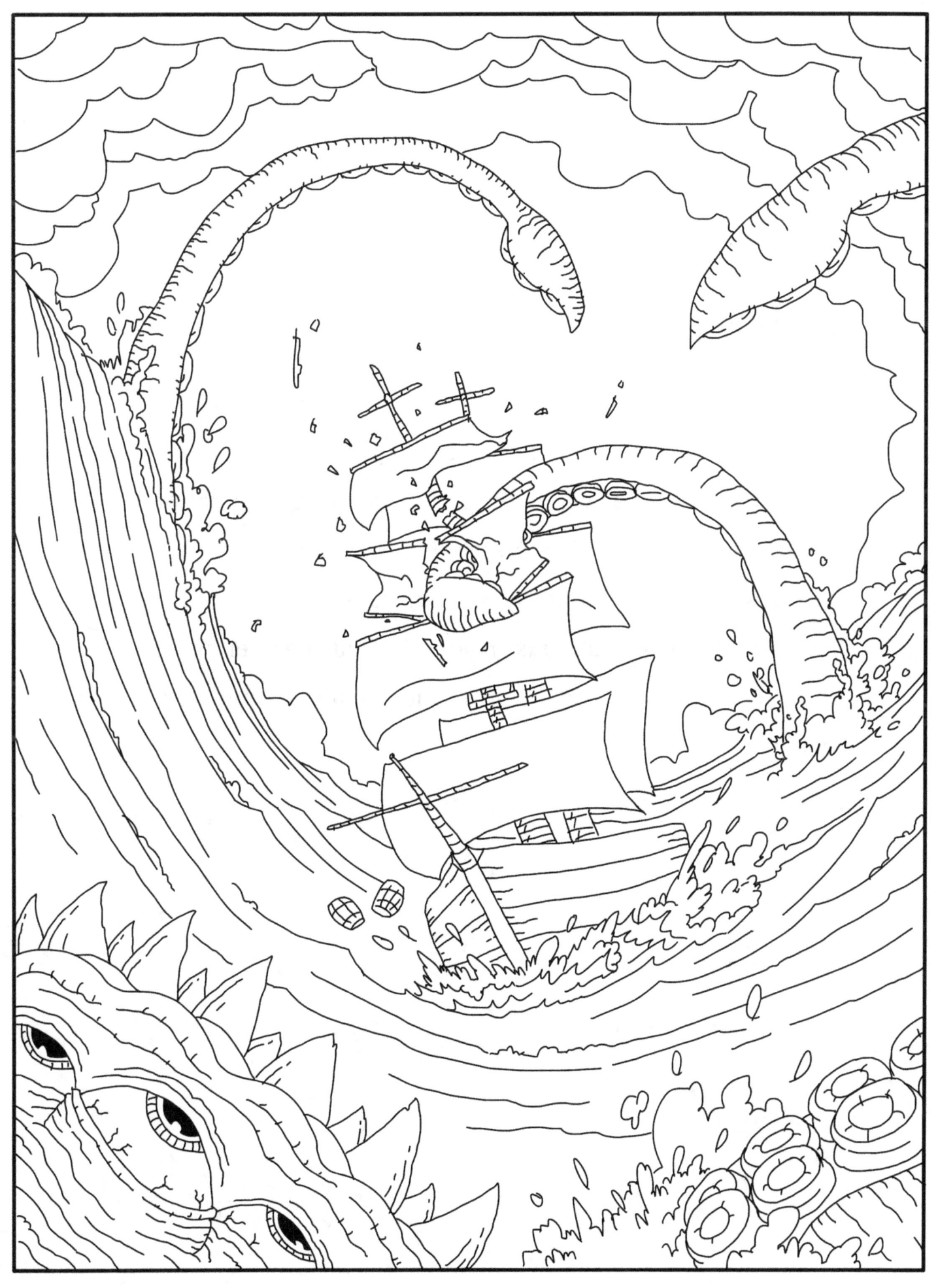

Medusa

Greek myths will always have a special place in my heart because they exude over-the-top creativity and imagination. Take Medusa, for example. Here's a woman with a face so hideous it will turn you to stone if you gaze upon it. And her hair is a bunch of venomous snakes. Oh, and she later gave birth to Pegasus (a winged horse) and a Giant, but only after being beheaded by Perseus.

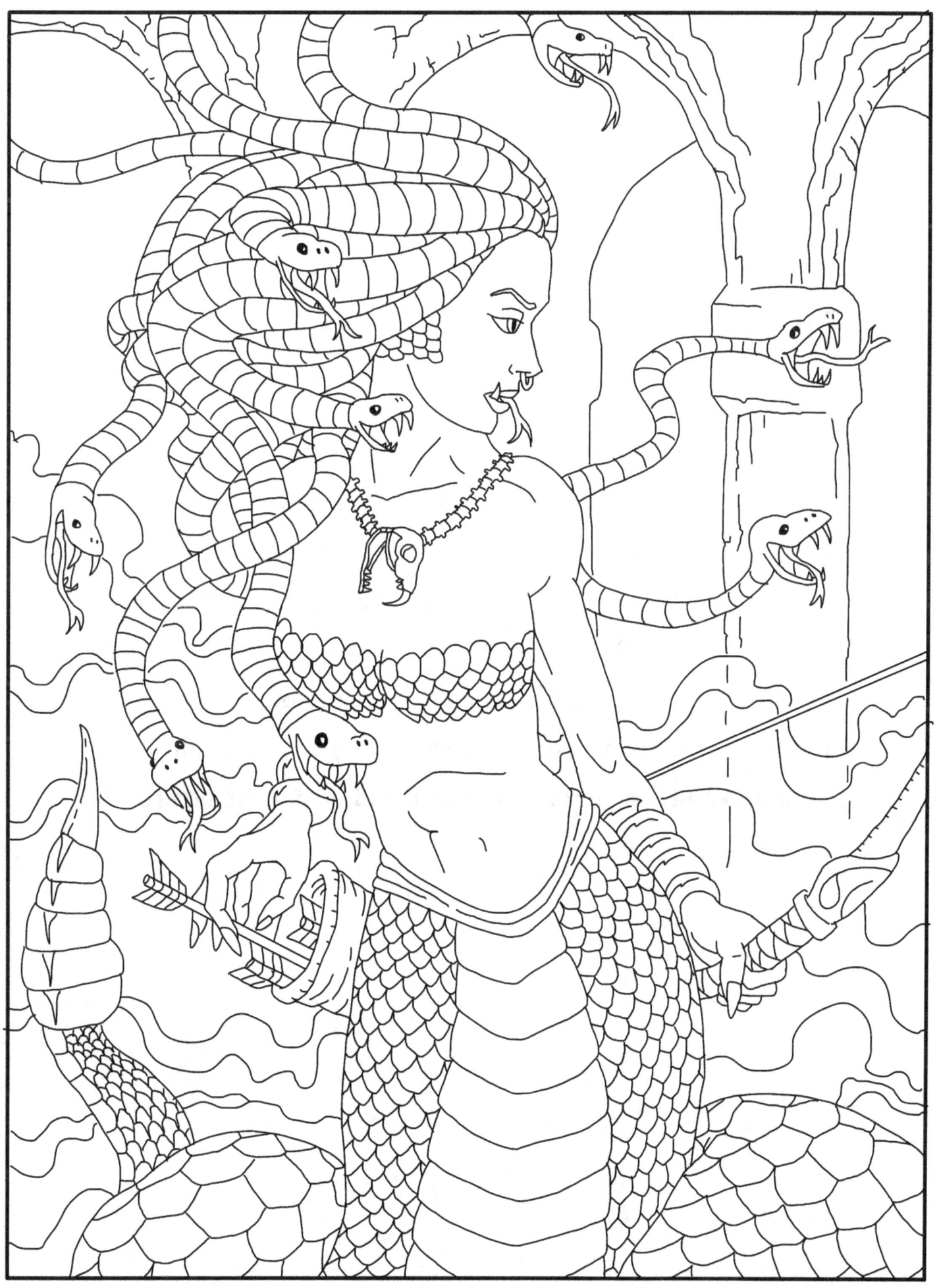

Mothman

The Mothman has been described by witnesses as a "large flying man with ten-foot wings" and glowing red eyes. In the late 1960s there were a rash of sightings in West Virginia leading up to the tragic collapse of the Silver Bridge, which claimed 46 lives. This gave rise to the legend that the Mothman's appearance was some sort of premonition or warning of the looming disaster. The Mothman is the only creature known to be concerned about failing infrastructure.

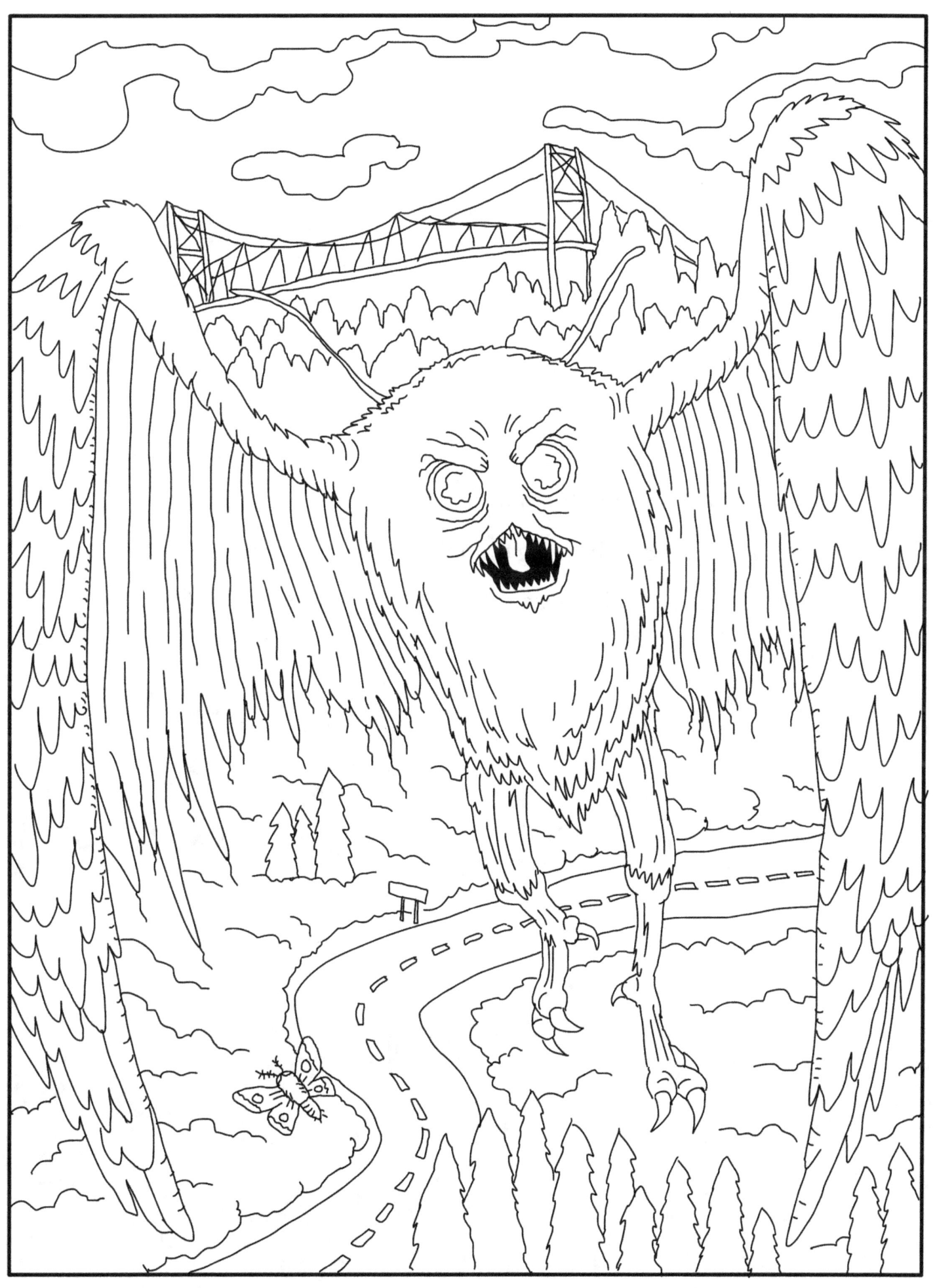

Globsters

Globsters – large, stinking, unidentifiable animal carcasses that wash ashore – are the Rorschach inkblot tests of cryptozoology. Beach-going onlookers can see whatever creature they want in these masses of decomposing flesh.

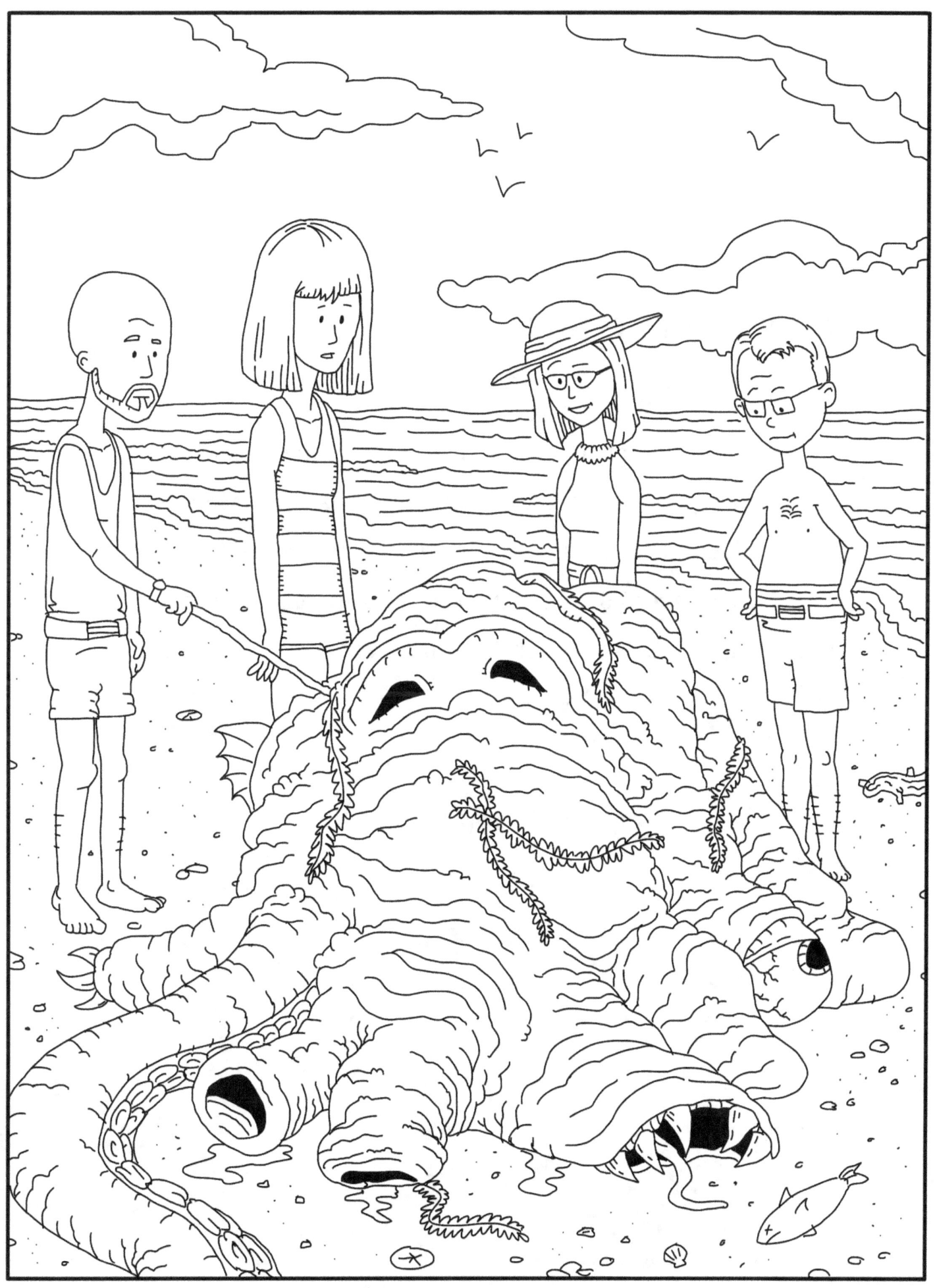

Mokele-mbembe

Mokele-mbembe means "one who stops the flow of rivers" and is the name given to a giant sauropod that hangs out in the Congo River basin. Local tribes have reported Mokele-mbembe sightings for over 200 years but the creature has never been photographed. Classic cryptid, being all elusive and whatnot.

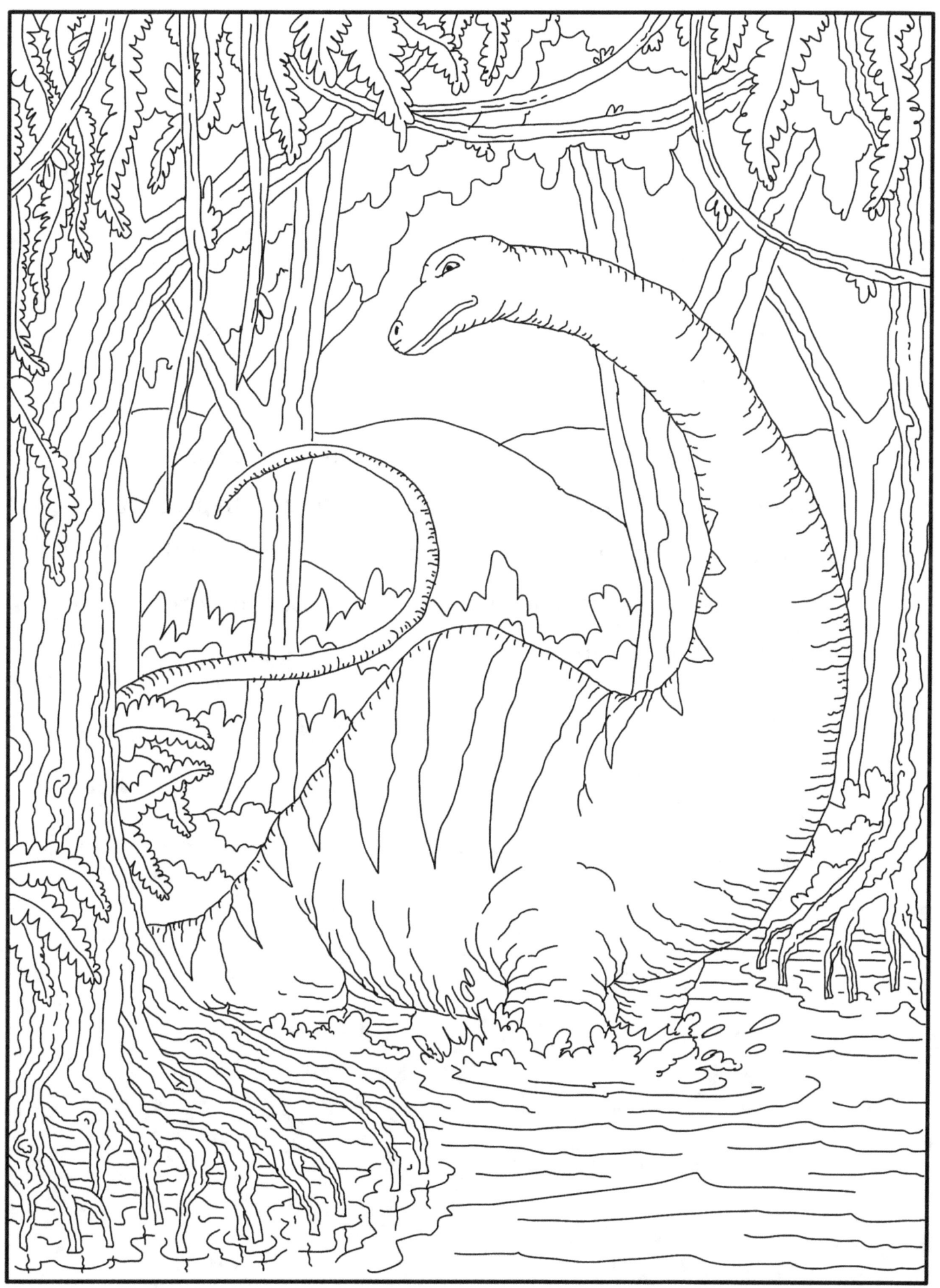

Fatbergs

Fatbergs are formed in sewers when cooking fat and wet wipes stick together in large lumps. They are the ultimate byproduct of human wastefulness. Fatbergs might sound gross, but they actually have big hearts and just want to explore the world outside of the drainpipes.

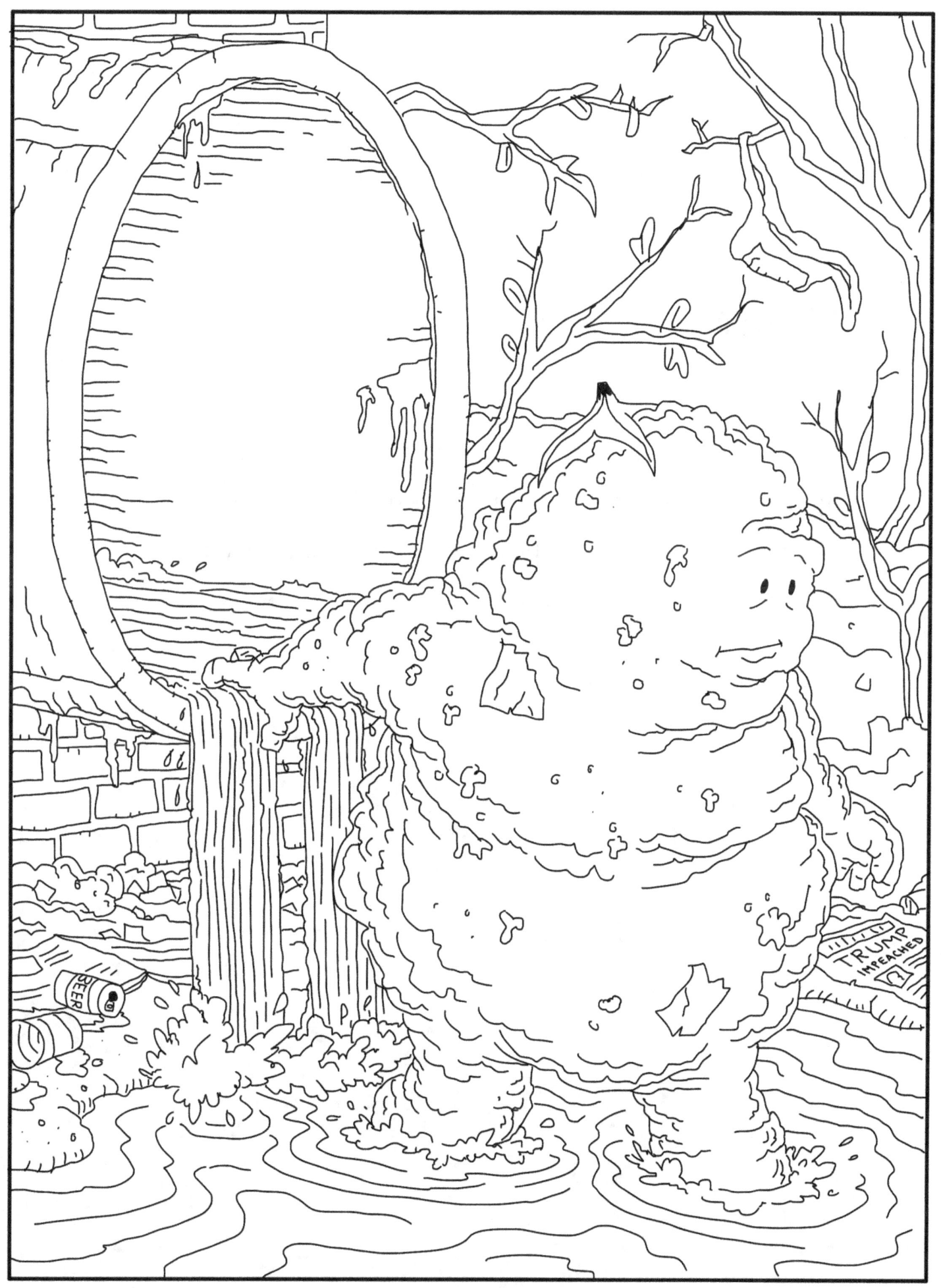

Little Green Men

Extraterrestrials have been on Earth for a while, abducting humans and performing experiments on them. But don't worry. They only seem to be interested in probing truck drivers on desolate highways.

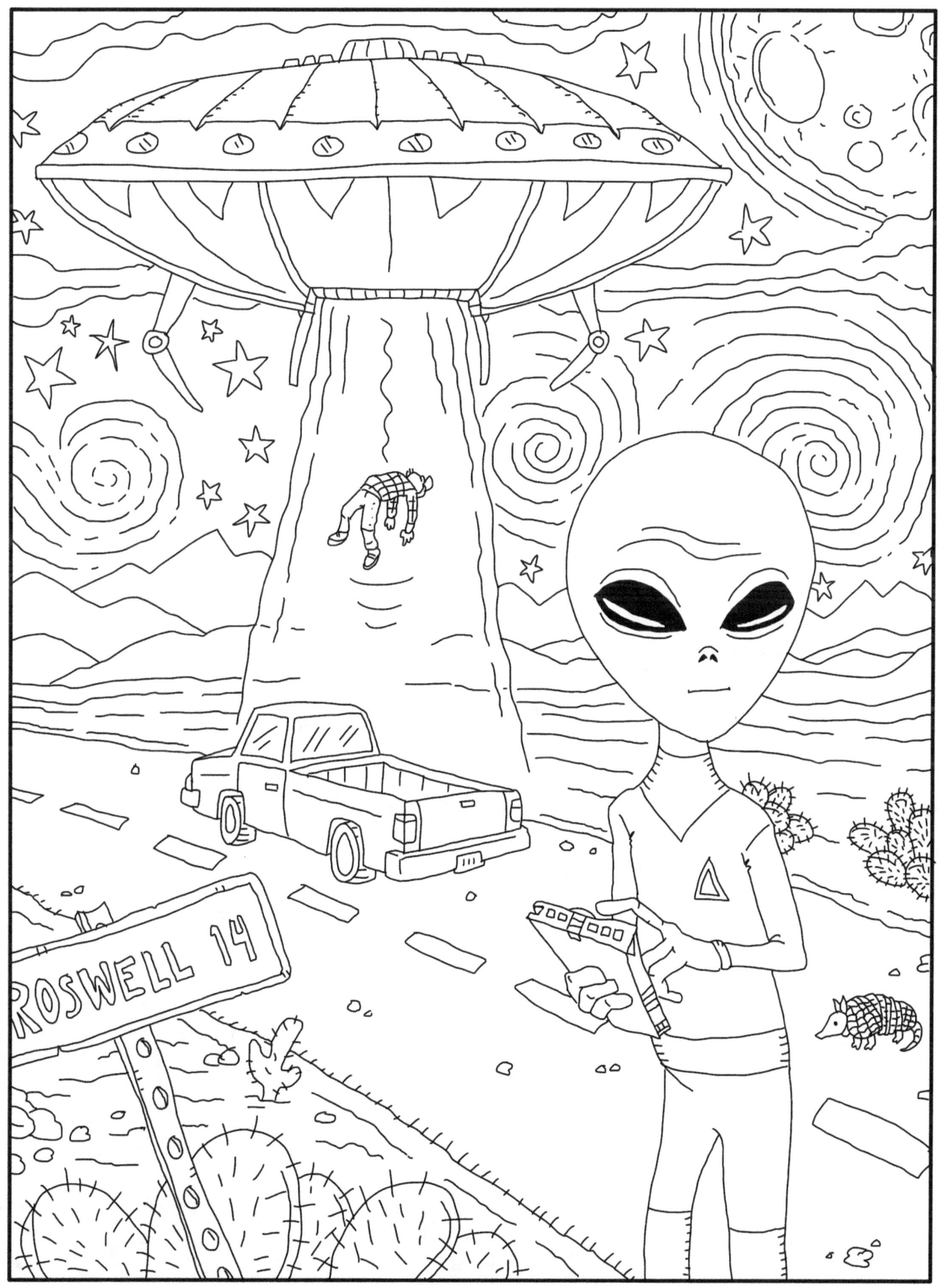